Love Overcomes Grief

Dan Widrich

A Word of Thanks

I wish to thank my mother, Lynn Widrich, for her patience and guidance in helping me to deal with the death of my father, for the countless hours that she spent listening to my ideas and for her help in editing and publishing this book; to my step-father, David Greenstein, for making helpful practical suggestions; to Stephen M. Robinson Ph.D. for his insight and encouragement; to David Allen for his invaluable computer expertise that made it possible to publish this book and to my family for their ongoing support. I would also like to give special recognition to my grandmother, the late Ruth Greenstein, for the artistic illustrations that she created for this book.

Dedication

This book is dedicated in loving memory of my father, Dr. Warren C. Widrich MD. His love of life, compassion for others, his devotion to family, to writing, and to teaching, inspired me to write this book.

Biographical Sketch

I became interested in writing after my father, Dr. Warren C. Widrich died. He was critically ill for two years, and during that time he was in and out of hospitals until his death in January 1988. I was only six and a half years old when he died. Since then, many other people close to me have also died. These experiences have given me empathy and insight into how children feel when faced with adversity.

The first step in the healing process was writing this book for children who have lost a parent. I started writing the book when I was seven and a half years old, though I had to stop for many years because the memories were too painful. Over the years I thought about how my life had changed, and once again I began to put my thoughts down on paper. To write a book that would help children adjust to this difficult situation was a dream of mine.

This year I was finally able to finish editing the book and make my dream a reality. The task was especially difficult for me because I had a traumatic birth history. That trauma left me with many learning disabilities and made both learning and emotional issues a major challenge.

In this passage through the Stages of Grief, I began to concentrate on other things that helped fulfill my life. With time I was able to develop new interests. Setting goals for myself helped me look toward the future. I learned how to drive a car, graduated Cum Laude from Mount Ida College, started doing community service with the elderly and began helping children with special needs. When I became aware of how fragile life is, I began researching my family tree and arranging family reunions. I am now known as the family historian. Now I enjoy writing, playing tennis, going to theater, taking part in trivia contests, and collecting decks of playing cards and Hard Rock Café "City" T-shirts. I continue to participate in many charity walks and also love traveling in the United States and abroad.

It is my hope that reading this book will be as therapeutic for you and your family as it has been for me to write. This book not only explains death in a way that young children can understand, but it also gives children and parents activities that will facilitate discussion and help the healing begin.

A Note to Parents

When your child asks you about the death of a loved one, it is a good idea to talk in a place where the child feels safe. It is important to make sure that you are not rushed. Be truthful, patient and be aware that you might be asked the same question many times. If you have trouble answering a question, it is fine to respond by saying, "that is a good question, and I will find the answer for you."

Each person grieves in his own way, and there is no set time when a person begins to feel better. Death is not an easy concept to explain. However, it is very important for the family to be able to talk about their feelings openly and honestly. There are several stages that a person goes through during the grieving period. By being aware of these stages, it will help you to understand the feelings that you and your children are going through.

SHOCK – This is the first stage of grieving when the person feels numb. Your child's body might have strange sensations such as butterflies in the stomach, and your child might not have much appetite.

DENIAL – This is the time when your child begins to understand what has happened but continues to act as if the loved one is still alive.

ANGER – In this stage a person who has lost someone often gets angry. He or she may blame the person who died for leaving. Anger may also be directed at the person who was responsible for care of the loved one. If the family practices a religion, the person can show anger towards God or simply grow angry for being left alone. Your child might become more easily annoyed with little things that normally would not bother a person.

GUILT and DEPRESSION – This is when a person questions himself, "could I have done anything differently? What if? If only I..." It is a time when your child might want to be alone and not do anything. Eventually with the help of friends, family and/or a professional counselor, the last stage of ACCEPTANCE will come.

ACCEPTANCE – This is the stage where the depression, anger and guilt are no longer present and when the person is able to talk or think about his/her feelings more objectively. It is a time when the person realizes that it is possible to still enjoy the activities that used to be pleasurable.

These stages are a natural part of the grieving process. The most helpful thing to remember is that it can take each person a different amount of time to pass through each stage. Allowing your child to express feelings will enable the healing process to take place.

For those who have lost a significant person, it can be difficult to realize the future will bring hope and healing. To help fill the void, there will come a time when those who are grieving begin to think about the important people in their lives. It could be an aunt, uncle, grandparent, neighbor, friend, counselor/psychologist, teacher, religious leader, a big brother or sister, or even a new step-parent. This is what happened to me. There were many good friends and relatives that helped me through the difficult period after the loss of my father, and I began to develop several new interests. Once again I began to enjoy and appreciate what life had to offer.

Hi, my name is Dan and I want to share my feelings with you about something that was and still is very hard for me to understand. The death of people whom I loved was very difficult. I am telling you my story because I have learned many things that have helped me to accept and understand my sadness.

On page 46 there is a list of activities that helped me feel better. You can also do them to help you work through your feelings about the death of your special person. In the back of this book on page 53 there is a Glossary that will explain unfamiliar words.

When I was six and a half years old, my dad died; and a year and a half later my great-grandmother died. They were my best friends. The death of these two very special people made me sad. When my dad and great-grandmother died, I was very unhappy, felt all alone, and my whole world seemed to be falling apart.

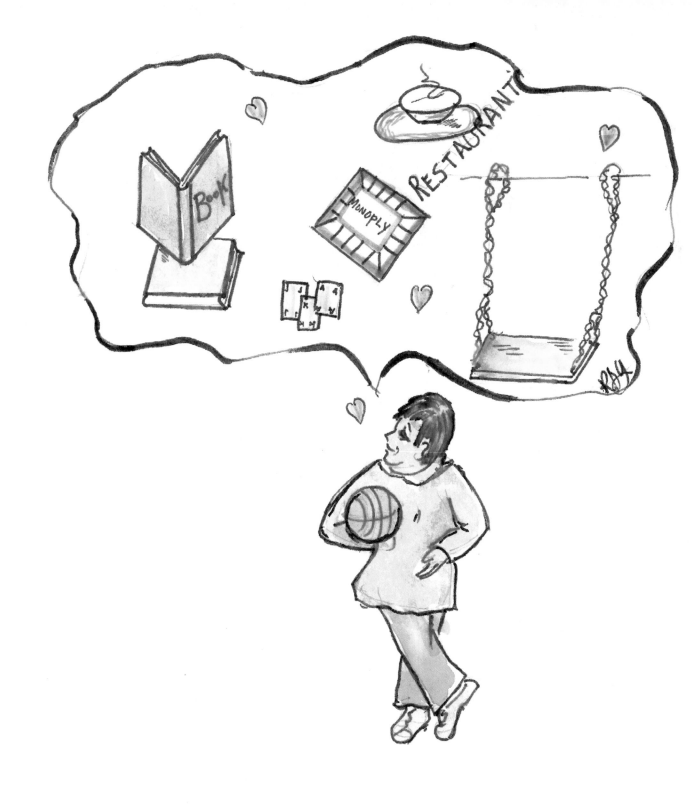

After awhile, the sad and angry feelings that I had all of the time began to lessen; and I was able to go on with my life. I started remembering many of the happy times and the special things that I did with my dad. We enjoyed playing Monopoly, going to the park where he pushed me on the swings, setting up and running my first electric train set, reading bedtime stories, and he even taught me how to climb on the jungle gym in the back yard.

I also remember the many nights that I slept over at my great-grandmother's apartment. We had so much fun playing the card games she taught me. When I was three years old, she thought I was grown up enough to eat in restaurants and took me out to eat every week.

In the beginning, thinking about these wonderful times used to upset me. Now I am able to remember how much fun I had with my dad and my great-grandmother without being so sad.

After the death of each person who was special to me, my mother suggested making a picture book of my memories. On each page she helped me to write down a thought that I remembered, or an activity I did, with that special person. Then I drew a picture. We put the pages together with a spiral binding. These became my very own books about the special people who had died.

I look at these books often, and it helps to bring back wonderful memories. You can do this too. On the next page write about a time that you enjoyed spending with your special person. Then draw the picture.

I remember when ...

_____

_____

_____

_____

_____

_____

Here is my picture:

When my dad and great-grandmother died, it was very important for me to talk with someone about the different feelings I had. It was hard for me to understand why the people I loved had to die. However, talking about my feelings with people who cared helped me feel better.

Some people you can talk to about these special feelings are: family members, friends, teachers, counselors, psychologists, psychiatrists, religious leaders and other people that you trust and feel comfortable talking with.

Sad thoughts went through my mind. It seemed that my dad did not love me anymore because he wasn't around to play with me. I also wondered what I had done wrong and asked myself why he wanted to leave me.

It was difficult for me to understand that his death didn't have anything to do with me and that it wasn't my fault. I couldn't do anything to keep my dad from dying. He didn't want to die. He was just too sick to live.

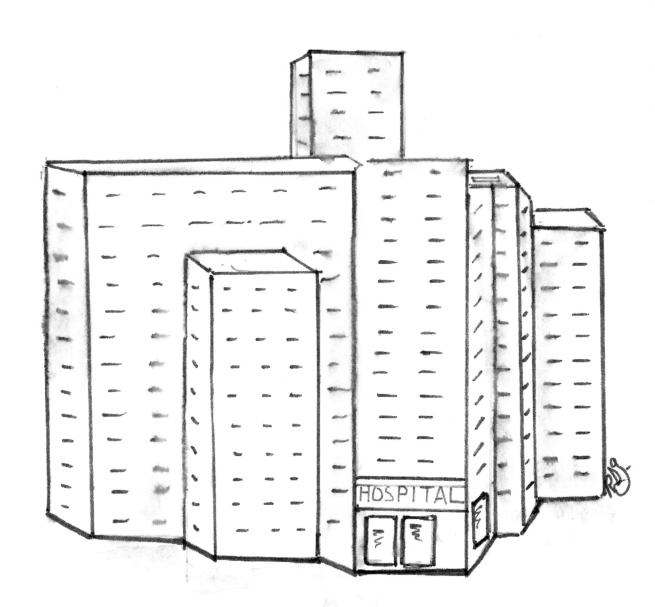

People that you love can die anywhere.

Some of the places that people can die are:

in a car

at work

at home

in a restaurant

and even in a hospital.

My dad died in a hospital

and

my great-grandmother died in a restaurant.

We all have different experiences with death.

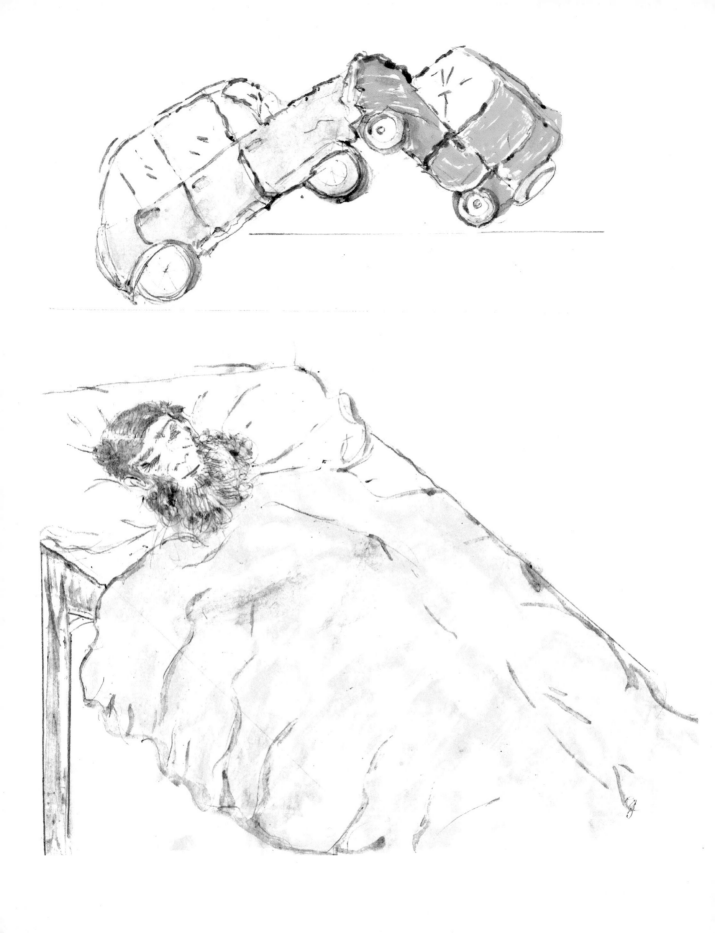

There are many reasons why people die. Some people get very sick like my dad. Other people have accidents that damage the body so much it can't be fixed. Many people die of old age. When people are old, the parts of the body get worn out and cannot work anymore. For example, since my great-grandmother was old, her heart wore out and just stopped working. When this happened, she died.

Some people are sick and live with pain for a long time. When my Dad died, I was very sad. Later I found out that he was always in a lot of pain and could no longer do many of the things that he enjoyed. This helped me to understand why he died.

With my great-grandmother it was different because she was very old and died suddenly. She had a heart attack, and it was over so fast that she never felt any pain. This was hard for me because I had no warning that something was wrong. She wasn't sick and seemed so healthy.

I know that the doctors and nurses did everything they could to try and help my father get better. Sometimes even doctors and nurses cannot do anything to help.

People die at different ages.

Some die young because they get very sick or are in an accident. Yet others live to be very old.

My father got sick and died when he was only 50 years old.

However, my great-grandmother was 92 years old and died after she had lived a long life.

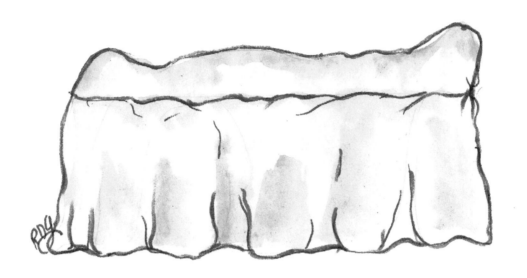

A person who has a serious accident or gets sick is usually taken to the hospital. If the person dies, he or she is carefully wrapped in a sheet. The body is then taken to a special place in the hospital called a morgue. This is where the body stays while the family makes arrangements with the funeral home. The people from the funeral home place the body into a special car called a hearse to transport the body.

The funeral home gives the body a bath and dresses him or her in the clothes that the family wants their loved one to be buried in. Usually a man is in a suit and tie, and a women is in a dress. This is because the family wants to be able to remember their loved one looking his or her best. Sometimes the family chooses a favorite outfit the person enjoyed wearing. The body is then placed in a special box called a casket or coffin.

Some families choose to have their loved ones cremated. This means the body is taken to a crematorium, turned into ashes, and then placed in an urn. The ashes can be scattered at a favorite spot, buried, or kept in an urn at home. In each case a memorial service is held to honor and remember the person who died.

After a person dies, the body lies so still that it looks like the person is just sleeping.

But this is different.

The person will not wake up or respond to anything, like noise or light.

When a person dies, the body can no longer
breathe,
touch,
feel,
smell,
or
move
as the person could while alive.

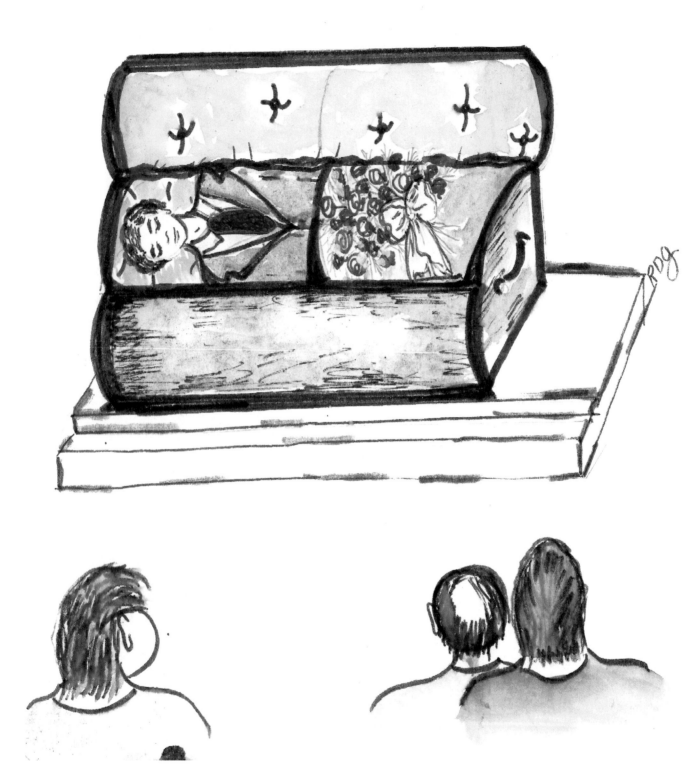

There are different types of ceremonies depending upon the family's religion or culture.

In the Christian religion, there is a wake the evening before the funeral. The wake takes place in the funeral home where, most of the time, people are able to see the body in the open casket. At the wake family and friends get together in order to comfort and support one another.

In the Jewish religion, people come together at the funeral. Before the funeral begins, usually only the immediate family and close relatives go into the chapel to view the open casket. Since the deceased person can no longer choose who views him or her, the Jewish tradition shows this special respect. That is why no one else sees the body in the open casket.

The funeral is a time for people to say a final good-bye to the special person who died. It is also a time to comfort the family. Many people take time off from work or school to attend the funeral. Some people travel from very far away.

A funeral can take place in a church, a synagogue, or in a funeral home. There may be flowers, music, and prayers. The people who say the prayers are called Clergy. In the Jewish religion that person is called a Rabbi. In the Christian religion the person is called a Priest or a Minister and is often referred to as "Father." At the funeral, family and sometimes a close friend will deliver a eulogy. These people speak in front of family and friends to share their special memories about the person who died.

After the funeral service the casket is placed in a hearse. This time the hearse transports the casket to the cemetery.

Family and friends get into the cars they came in. The cars form a line that is called a funeral procession. The religious leader travels in the first car. Then the hearse follows.

The immediate family usually rides in a limousine that travels behind the hearse. They ride in a limousine so that they do not have to worry about driving while they are upset. This is time they can spend talking together.

Have you every seen a line of cars
going down the street that have
their headlights and flashers on
during the day?

All of the vehicles that are in the funeral procession have their headlights and flashers on. They have either a funeral procession banner on the dashboard or a flag attached to the outside of the car. This tells the other cars on the road it is a funeral and that these cars need to follow each other. When drivers in the other cars see this, they know not to interrupt by breaking into line. The procession passes first, and then the other cars on the road can go.

The procession of cars enters the cemetery. This is a quiet and peaceful place surrounded by grass and trees. Everyone gets out of the cars and gathers around the grave. The religious leader then recites some prayers. This is called a service.

In the Jewish religion, family and friends stay in their cars until the casket is lowered into the ground. Then they walk to the grave. After the service, family members sometimes throw a flower on top of the casket before relatives and friends scatter a small shovel of dirt into the open grave. The back part of the shovel is used to pick up the dirt. It is done this way to show that the shovel is being used differently. This is considered an act of love and respect for the deceased person. Afterwards everyone leaves the cemetery and gathers at the home of the deceased or at a family member's house. It is a time when friends keep the family company. Food is put out for everyone to eat.

In the Christian religion, people get out of their cars immediately and walk to the grave. After the service they place a flower on the casket while it is still on top of the ground. When people get back into their cars and leave the cemetery, the casket is lowered into the ground. In order to spend time with each other, family and close friends then usually go out to eat.

In the Jewish religion the family sits Shiva for several days after the funeral. This takes place either at the house of the person who has died or at the home of one of the relatives. Family and friends come together to comfort each other, to express their sadness, and also to remember the good and special times they had with the person. At the house there are usually drinks and desserts for people to eat.

Since my Dad is buried in a cemetery, there are times that I want to visit his grave. It makes me feel close to him.

It is a private time when I think about the good times that we shared together. This is when I tell my Dad I am keeping all of the promises he asked me to make. I share with him the new things that I am doing.

When I go to the cemetery, I also bring flowers to put on his grave. These are some of the ways I show my love and respect for him. I think about how proud he would be to see the young man I have turned out to be.

Sharing thoughts

Remembering

It was such a sad time for me when people I loved died. I wondered what would help me feel better.

My mother and I thought about the different things that could help me express my feelings. You can find these activities on page 46.

After doing some of these projects, I started to feel better. Then I realized I could remember the good times I shared with my dad and with my great-grandmother without feeling so sad.

The happy and sad experiences people have in life make them stronger. This means they are learning to understand what life is about and how to cope with difficult experiences.

I have learned that it is okay to cry and to have strong feelings when sad things happen. There will be times when you will feel sad, especially when you think about the important people in your life who have died. These feelings may last for a long time.   This is part of the normal grieving process.

There was an important lesson I had to learn when my father and great-grandmother died. At times I had to put my sad feelings aside so that I could do my schoolwork and play with my friends. That didn't mean that I should forget about them or not feel sad. But there were times I had to concentrate on doing other things.

Even though I missed my dad and great-grandmother very much, I found out that it was okay to have happy thoughts too. These people will always be a part of me, and I will always have a special place in my heart for them.

Death is a natural part of life. All living things such as
trees, plants, animals and people will die someday.
If nothing died, there would not be enough food or
places for all of the people, animals and plants. This
means that the earth would become overcrowded.
When I think about this, it helps me to understand why
people and all living things have to die.

If you have a friend whose parent or loved one died, please tell the person to read my book. I hope it will help you and other children understand that people have many different feelings when someone they love dies.

Death just happens, and it is not anyone's fault.

My dad taught me that some people are luckier than others. I guess that is really true because some people live for a long time while others die at a young age.

When you think about the special people who have died, their love, and the wonderful memories you have made with these people will always comfort you.

Are there any words or ideas in this book that you do not understand?

Please ask a person that you trust to explain it to you. That person will be able to answer your questions and help you understand your feelings.

When you are able to share your feelings with others, you will begin to feel better.

As you grow older, the memories of the good times you had with that special person will bring you happy thoughts instead of sad ones.

I hope that after reading this book and doing the activities found on the next page, you will feel better.

Remember, there are many people who have feelings just like you.

THINGS TO DO THAT WILL HELP YOU FEEL BETTER

1. Try to write down or talk to someone that you trust about something that makes you happy. This is called positive thinking.

2. Draw a picture of the special person who died.

3. Write a letter to the special person in your life who died and tell him or her all the things you would like the person to know.

4. The next time you visit the cemetery where your special person is buried, make a card to leave on the grave.

5. Make a book about your special person. On each page write about something you remember doing with that person. You may also want to draw a picture about this event.

6. Look at pictures, videos or anything else that reminds you of the happy times you spent with that special person.

7. Do some of the same things that you used to enjoy with your special person. This will help you remember the good times that you had together.

8. Have fun with your friends and family. Enjoy today because that special person would want you to be happy.

9. Re-read this book to help you understand you are not alone. That will help you review new things you have learned from the book.

10. Read the book that you made (see suggestion # 5) about the special person who died. It will help you remember the wonderful times you had together.

Here is one of my favorite pictures: my great grandmother Doree, my father Warren, my mother Lynn, and me when I was 5 years old.

After talking with people I trusted and doing the activities in this book, I began to feel better. Then I noticed good things in my life started to happen.

Five years after my father died, my mother met a wonderful person named David Greenstein; and they got married. David's mother, Ruth Greenstein, became my grandmother. She was a very talented artist and is the person who illustrated this book.

I mentioned both of these people in "A Word of Thanks" at the beginning of this book. On the next page is a picture of both my step-father, David, and his mother (my grandmother), Ruth.

I feel lucky to be part of my new family.

This is a picture of my step-father, David,
and his mother Ruth, my grandmother, who
drew the pictures for this book.

Grandpa Arthur and I at my
College Graduation

The ACTIVITIES in this book WORKED for ME again.

After my Dad died, my Grandpa Arthur became the person I turned to for advice. He was very loving, caring, and supportive, a person I could always count on. Despite the fact that he lived far away, we spoke on the phone almost every day.

This summer it felt like my world fell apart when my very special Grandpa died at age 93. Devastated, I read this book again and did some of the activities listed on page 46. This helped to ease my pain. I hope reading this book will help you too.

GLOSSARY

A

Ashes - Powdery matter remaining after cremation

B

Bury - To put in the ground and cover with earth

C

Casket - A box or container that is made of metal or wood and is lined with cloth or satin. This is what the body is usually buried in.

Cemetery - A quiet place where your loved one is buried

Church - A place of worship for Christians

Clergy - A Rabbi, Minister, or Priest

Coffin - The same as a casket but the word is mostly used in Europe

Cremation - An alternate option to burial where the body is turned into ashes

D

Death - The end of someone's life

Deceased - Dead

Dying – When someone is very sick and the body is having a hard time functioning

E

Eulogy - A speech delivered at a funeral by a relative or a close friend who shares special memories about the person who died

F

Funeral - A ceremony for a dead person prior to burial

Funeral Home - A building where your loved one is taken after he or she has died. The funeral home will dress the person before placing the body into the casket. The wake is usually held in the funeral home and sometimes a funeral service is also held there. This is the place where you get to see your loved one for the last time.

Funeral Procession – A line of cars that follow the hearse from the funeral home or the place of worship to the cemetery

G

Grave - A hole in the ground about 6 feet deep that the casket or urn is put into

H

Hearse - A special car that transports the body to the funeral home and then to the place of burial

Hospital - A place where sick or injured people are given medical and surgical treatment

I

Immediate Family - Relatives consisting of parents, grandparents, brothers, sisters and spouses

L

Limousine - A large car owned by the funeral home that the family rides in

M

Morgue - A place in the hospital where your loved one who died is taken until arrangements can be made to transport the body to the funeral home

Mortuary - Another name for a funeral home

P

Procession - A line of cars carrying family and friends that are going to the cemetery

R

Rabbi - A Jewish religious leader

Religion - A set of beliefs and practices generally agreed on by a group of people

S

Service – A religious ceremony

Shiva - In the Jewish religion, Shiva begins immediately after the burial and lasts for one to seven days. The length of Shiva depends upon the religious beliefs and the deceased's wishes. It is a time when family and friends go to the home of the person who died or to a close relative's home. They visit with and comfort the immediate family. A candle burns for the seven days of mourning.

Synagogue - A place where Jewish people pray and meet for religious instruction

T

Transport - To bring from one place to another

U

Urn - A small box or vase where ashes of the body are kept after cremation

W

Wake – In the Christian Religion, this is a time where family and friends meet at the funeral home to talk to each other and to give each other support. The casket is usually open so that people can see the body and say goodbye to the person who died.

Made in the USA
Monee, IL
13 March 2021